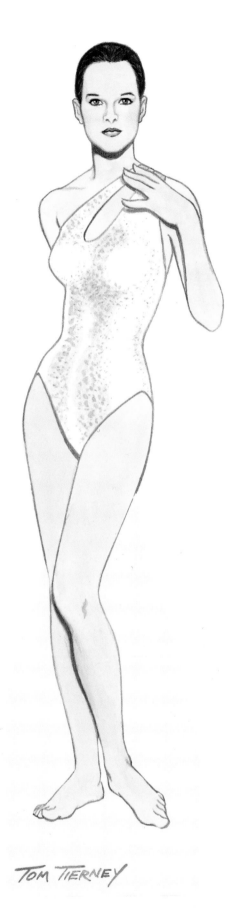

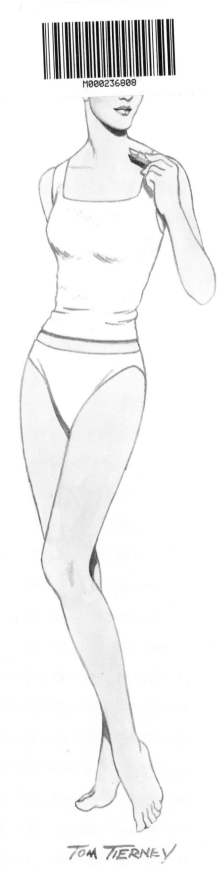

Tom Tierney

Tom Tierney

1998
House of Anne Klein
swimsuit

1998
House of Anne Cole
underwear

PLATE 1

1990
Emanuel Ungaro
Lamé evening gown

1990
Christian Lacroix
Patterned silk ensemble

PLATE 2

1990
Geoffrey Beene
Silk jacquard evening ensemble

1991
Oscar de la Renta
Silk shantung dress and coat

PLATE 3

1991
Valentino
Bell-skirted evening ensemble

1991
Todd Oldham
Patchwork plaid suit

PLATE 4

do not cut out
white spaces between
arms and bodies

1992
Arnold Scaasi
Polka dot strapless crepe dress

1992
Michael Kors
Short strapless dress and cardigan

PLATE 5

do not cut out
white spaces between
arms and bodies

1992
Bob Mackie
Velvet and taffeta evening gown

1993
Bill Blass
Knit tube dress

PLATE 6

1993
Linda Allard for Ellen Tracy
Pin-stripe suit

1993
Adolfo
Polka dot print ensemble

PLATE 7

1994
Nina Ricci
Pleated silk gown

1994
Louis Féraud
Evening gown with capelike collar

PLATE 8

1994
Jean-Louis Scherrer
Minidress ball gown

1995
Gianfranco Ferré
Classic suit and topcoat

PLATE 9

do not cut out
white spaces between
arms and bodies

1995
Thierry Mugler
Miniskirted suit and vinyl pants

1995
Vera Wang
Corset-bodice ball gown

PLATE 10

1996
Carolina Herrera
Satin wedding suit

1996
Donna Karan
Body-hugging silk knit tube dress

PLATE 11

1996
Norma Kamali
Panne velvet lamb-trimmed ensemble

1997
Isaac Mizrahi
Plunging-neckline tailored suit

PLATE 12

1997
Giorgio Armani
Unstructured great coat
and full-cut pants

1997
Gianni Versace
Slinky silk knit evening gown

PLATE 13

1998
John Galliano for Dior
"Scheherazade" kimono and gown

1998
Karl Lagerfeld for Chanel
Sequined tulle dress

PLATE 14

1998
Alexander McQueen for Givenchy
Wool coat with gray fox collar

1999
Ralph Lauren
Cashmere sweater with satin ball skirt

PLATE 15